DATABASE
MANAGEMENT SYSTEMS
DMBS

By MOHAMMED ZAHID WADIWALE

Learning Simply Made Easy

About the book

Database Management System or DBMS in short refers to the technology of storing and retrieving users' data with utmost efficiency along with appropriate security measures. DBMS allows its users to create their own databases as per their requirement. These databases are highly configurable and offer a bunch of options.

This book explains the basics of DBMS such as its architecture, data models, data schemas, data independence, E-R model, relation model, relational database design, and storage and file structure. In addition, it covers a few advanced topics such as indexing and hashing, transaction and concurrency, and backup and recovery.

Audience

This book will especially help computer science graduates in understanding the basic-to-advanced concepts related to Database Management Systems.

Prerequisites

Before you start proceeding with this book, it is recommended that you have a good understanding of basic computer concepts such as primary memory, secondary memory, and data structures and algorithms.

Index

1. OVERVIEW

Database is a collection of related data and data is a collection of facts and figures that can be processed to produce information.

Mostly data represents recordable facts. Data aids in producing information, which is based on facts. For example, if we have data about marks obtained by all students, we can then conclude about toppers and average marks.

A **database management system** stores data in such a way that it becomes easier to retrieve, manipulate, and produce information.

Characteristics

Traditionally, data was organized in file formats. DBMS was a new concept then, and all the research was done to make it overcome the deficiencies in traditional style of data management. A modern DBMS has the following characteristics:

- **Real-world entity**: A modern DBMS is more realistic and uses real-world entities to design its architecture. It uses the behavior and attributes too. For example, a school database may use students as an entity and their age as an attribute.

- **Relation-based tables**: DBMS allows entities and relations among them to form tables. A user can understand the architecture of a database just by looking at the table names.

- **Isolation of data and application**: A database system is entirely different than its data. A database is an active entity, whereas data is said to be passive, on which the database works and organizes. DBMS also stores metadata, which is data about data, to ease its own process.

- **Less redundancy**: DBMS follows the rules of normalization, which splits a relation when any of its attributes is having redundancy in values. Normalization is a mathematically rich and scientific process that reduces data redundancy.

- **Consistency**: Consistency is a state where every relation in a database remains consistent. There exist methods and techniques, which can detect attempt of leaving database in inconsistent state. A DBMS can provide greater consistency as compared to earlier forms of data storing applications like file-processing systems.

- **Query Language**: DBMS is equipped with query language, which makes it more efficient to retrieve and manipulate data. A user can apply as many and as different filtering options as required to retrieve a set of data. Traditionally it was not possible where file-processing system was used.

- **ACID Properties**: DBMS follows the concepts of **A**tomicity, **C**onsistency, **I**solation, and **D**urability (normally shortened as ACID). These concepts are applied on transactions, which manipulate data in a database. ACID properties help the database stay healthy in multi-transactional environments and in case of failure.

- **Multiuser and Concurrent Access**: DBMS supports multi-user environment and allows them to access and manipulate data in parallel. Though there are restrictions on transactions when users attempt to handle the same data item, but users are always unaware of them.

- **Multiple views**: DBMS offers multiple views for different users. A user who is in the Sales department will have a different view of database than a person working in the Production department. This feature enables the users to have a concentrate view of the database according to their requirements.

- **Security**: Features like multiple views offer security to some extent where users are unable to access data of other users and departments. DBMS offers methods to impose constraints while entering data into the database and retrieving the same at a later stage. DBMS offers many different levels of security features, which enables multiple users to have different views with different features. For example, a user in the Sales department cannot see the data that belongs to the Purchase department. Additionally, it can also be managed how much data of the Sales department should be displayed to the user. Since a DBMS is not saved on the disk as traditional file systems, it is very hard for miscreants to break the code.

Users

A typical DBMS has users with different rights and permissions who use it for different purposes. Some users retrieve data and some back it up. The users of a DBMS can be broadly categorized as follows:

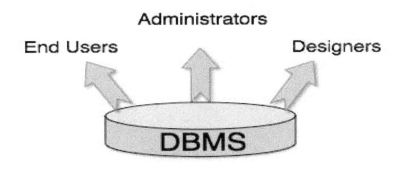

[*Image: DBMS Users*]

- **Administrators**: Administrators maintain the DBMS and are responsible for administrating the database. They are responsible to look after its usage and by whom it should be used. They create access profiles for users and apply limitations to maintain isolation and force security. Administrators also look after DBMS resources like system license, required tools, and other software and hardware related maintenance.

- **Designers**: Designers are the group of people who actually work on the designing part of the database. They keep a close watch on what data should be kept and in what format. They identify and design the whole set of entities, relations, constraints, and views.

- **End Users**: End users are those who actually reap the benefits of having a DBMS. End users can range from simple viewers who pay attention to the logs or market rates to sophisticated users such as business analysts.

2. ARCHITECTURE

The design of a DBMS depends on its architecture. It can be centralized or decentralized or hierarchical. The architecture of a DBMS can be seen as either single tier or multi-tier. An n-tier architecture divides the whole system into related but independent **n** modules, which can be independently modified, altered, changed, or replaced.

In 1-tier architecture, the DBMS is the only entity where the user directly sits on the DBMS and uses it. Any changes done here will directly be done on the DBMS itself. It does not provide handy tools for end-users. Database designers and programmers normally prefer to use single-tier architecture.

If the architecture of DBMS is 2-tier, then it must have an application through which the DBMS can be accessed. Programmers use 2-tier architecture where they access the DBMS by means of an application. Here the application tier is entirely independent of the database in terms of operation, design, and programming.

3-tier Architecture

A 3-tier architecture separates its tiers from each other based on the complexity of the users and how they use the data present in the database. It is the most widely used architecture to design a DBMS.

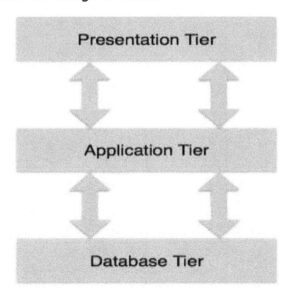

[*Image: 3-tier DBMS architecture*]

- **Database (Data) Tier**: At this tier, the database resides along with its query processing languages. We also have the relations that define the data and their constraints at this level.

- **Application (Middle) Tier**: At this tier reside the application server and the programs that access the database. For a user, this application tier presents an abstracted view of the database. End-users are unaware of any existence of the database beyond the application. At the other end, the database tier is not aware of any other user beyond the application tier. Hence, the application layer sits in the middle and acts as a mediator between the end-user and the database.

- **User (Presentation) Tier**: End-users operate on this tier and they know nothing about any existence of the database beyond this layer. At this layer, multiple views of the database can be provided by the application. All views are generated by applications that reside in the application tier.

Multiple-tier database architecture is highly modifiable, as almost all its components are independent and can be changed independently.

3. DATA MODELS

Data models define how the logical structure of a database is modeled. Data Models are fundamental entities to introduce abstraction in a DBMS. Data models define how data is connected to each other and how they are processed and stored inside the system.

The very first data model could be flat data-models, where all the data used are to be kept in the same plane. Earlier data models were not so scientific, hence they were prone to introduce lots of duplication and update anomalies.

Entity-Relationship Model

Entity-Relationship (ER) Model is based on the notion of real-world entities and relationships among them. While formulating real-world scenario into the database model, the ER Model creates entity set, relationship set, general attributes, and constraints.

ER Model is best used for the conceptual design of a database.

ER Model is based on:

- **Entities** and their attributes.

- **Relationships** among entities.

These concepts are explained below.

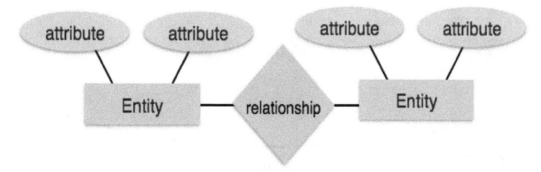

[*Image: ER Model*]

- **Entity**

    An entity in an ER Model is a real-world entity having properties called **attributes**. Every attribute is defined by its set of values called **domain**.

    For example, in a school database, a student is considered as an entity. Student has various attributes like name, age, class, etc.

- **Relationship**

The logical association among entities is called **relationship**. Relationships are mapped with entities in various ways. Mapping cardinalities define the number of association between two entities.

Mapping cardinalities:

- o   one to one

- o   one to many

- o   many to one

- o   many to many

Relational Model

The most popular data model in DBMS is the Relational Model. It is more scientific a model than others. This model is based on first-order predicate logic and defines a table as an **n-ary relation**.

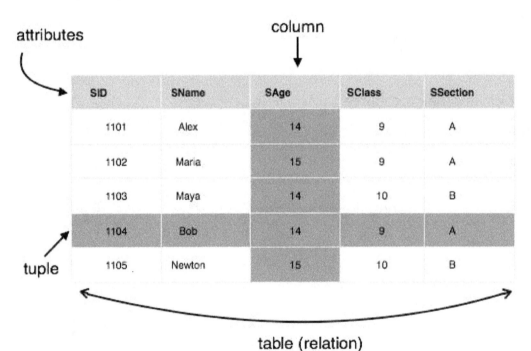

[*Image: Table in relational Model*]

The main highlights of this model are:

- Data is stored in tables called **relations**.

- Relations can be normalized.

- In normalized relations, values saved are atomic values.

- Each row in a relation contains a unique value.

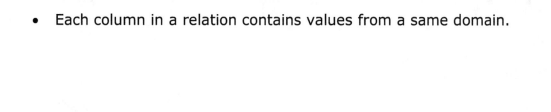

- Each column in a relation contains values from a same domain.

4. DATA SCHEMAS

Database Schema

A database schema is the skeleton structure that represents the logical view of the entire database. It defines how the data is organized and how the relations among them are associated. It formulates all the constraints that are to be applied on the data.

A database schema defines its entities and the relationship among them. It contains a descriptive detail of the database, which can be depicted by means of schema diagrams. It's the database designers who design the schema to help programmers understand the database and make it useful.

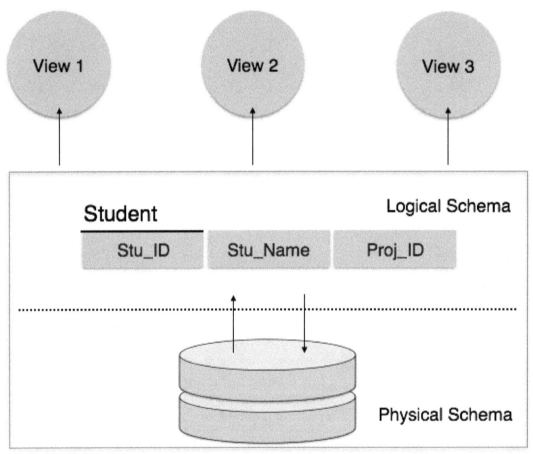

[*Image: Database Schemas*]

A database schema can be divided broadly into two categories:

- **Physical Database Schema**: This schema pertains to the actual storage of data and its form of storage like files, indices, etc. It defines how the data will be stored in a secondary storage.

- **Logical Database Schema**: This schema defines all the logical constraints that need to be applied on the data stored. It defines tables, views, and integrity constraints.

Database Instance

It is important that we distinguish these two terms individually. Database schema is the skeleton of database. It is designed when the database doesn't exist at all. Once the database is operational, it is very difficult to make any changes to it. A database schema does not contain any data or information.

A database instance is a state of operational database with data at any given time. It contains a snapshot of the database. Database instances tend to change with time. A DBMS ensures that its every instance (state) is in a valid state, by diligently following all the validations, constraints, and conditions that the database designers have imposed.

5. DATA INDEPENDENCE

If a database system is not multi-layered, then it becomes difficult to make any changes in the database system. Database systems are designed in multi-layers as we learnt earlier.

Data Independence

A database system normally contains a lot of data in addition to users' data. For example, it stores data about data, known as metadata, to locate and retrieve data easily. It is rather difficult to modify or update a set of metadata once it is stored in the database. But as a DBMS expands, it needs to change over time to satisfy the requirements of the users. If the entire data is dependent, it would become a tedious and highly complex job.

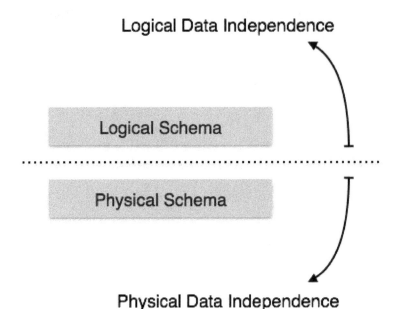

[*Image: Data independence*]

Metadata itself follows a layered architecture, so that when we change data at one layer, it does not affect the data at another level. This data is independent but mapped to each other.

Logical Data Independence

Logical data is data about database, that is, it stores information about how data is managed inside. For example, a table (relation) stored in the database and all its constraints applied on that relation.

Logical data independence is a kind of mechanism, which liberalizes itself from actual data stored on the disk. If we do some changes on table format, it should not change the data residing on the disk.

Physical Data Independence

All the schemas are logical, and the actual data is stored in bit format on the disk. Physical data independence is the power to change the physical data without impacting the schema or logical data.

For example, in case we want to change or upgrade the storage system itself — suppose we want to replace hard-disks with SSD — it should not have any impact on the logical data or schemas.

6. ER MODEL – BASIC CONCEPTS

The ER model defines the conceptual view of a database. It works around real-world entities and the associations among them. At view level, the ER model is considered a good option for designing databases.

Entity

An entity can be a real-world object, either animate or inanimate, that can be easily identifiable. For example, in a school database, students, teachers, classes, and courses offered can be considered as entities. All these entities have some attributes or properties that give them their identity.

An entity set is a collection of similar types of entities. An entity set may contain entities with attribute sharing similar values. For example, a Students set may contain all the students of a school; likewise a Teachers set may contain all the teachers of a school from all faculties. Entity sets need not be disjoint.

Attributes

Entities are represented by means of their properties called **attributes**. All attributes have values. For example, a student entity may have name, class, and age as attributes.

There exists a domain or range of values that can be assigned to attributes. For example, a student's name cannot be a numeric value. It has to be alphabetic. A student's age cannot be negative, etc.

Types of Attributes

- **Simple attribute:** Simple attributes are atomic values, which cannot be divided further. For example, a student's phone number is an atomic value of 10 digits.

- **Composite attribute:** Composite attributes are made of more than one simple attribute. For example, a student's complete name may have first_name and last_name.

- **Derived attribute:** Derived attributes are the attributes that do not exist in the physical database, but their values are derived from other attributes present in the database. For example, average_salary in a department should not be saved directly in the database, instead it can be derived. For another example, age can be derived from data_of_birth.

- **Single-value attribute:** Single-value attributes contain single value. For example: Social_Security_Number.

- **Multi-value attribute:** Multi-value attributes may contain more than one values. For example, a person can have more than one phone number, email_address, etc.

These attribute types can come together in a way like:

- simple single-valued attributes
- simple multi-valued attributes
- composite single-valued attributes
- composite multi-valued attributes

Entity-Set and Keys

Key is an attribute or collection of attributes that uniquely identifies an entity among entity set.

For example, the roll_number of a student makes him/her identifiable among students.

- **Super Key**: A set of attributes (one or more) that collectively identifies an entity in an entity set.

- **Candidate Key**: A minimal super key is called a candidate key. An entity set may have more than one candidate key.

- **Primary Key**: A primary key is one of the candidate keys chosen by the database designer to uniquely identify the entity set.

Relationship

The association among entities is called a relationship. For example, an employee **works_at** a department, a student **enrolls** in a course. Here, Works_at and Enrolls are called relationships.

Relationship Set

A set of relationships of similar type is called a relationship set. Like entities, a relationship too can have attributes. These attributes are called **descriptive attributes**.

Degree of Relationship

The number of participating entities in a relationship defines the degree of the relationship.

- Binary = degree 2

- Ternary = degree 3

- n-ary = degree

Mapping Cardinalities

Cardinality defines the number of entities in one entity set, which can be associated with the number of entities of other set via relationship set.

- **One-to-one**: One entity from entity set A can be associated with at most one entity of entity set B and vice versa.

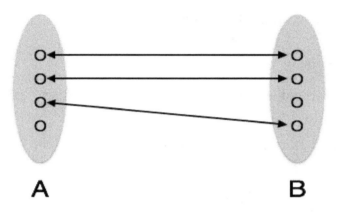

[Image: One-to-one relation]

- **One-to-many**: One entity from entity set A can be associated with more than one entities of entity set B, however an entity from entity set B can be associated with at most one entity.

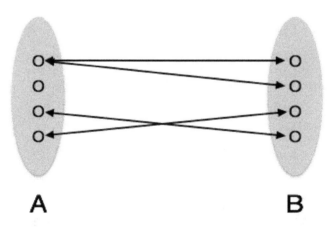

[Image: One-to-many relation]

- **Many-to-one**: More than one entities from entity set A can be associated with at most one entity of entity set B, however an entity from entity set B can be associated with more than one entity from entity set A.

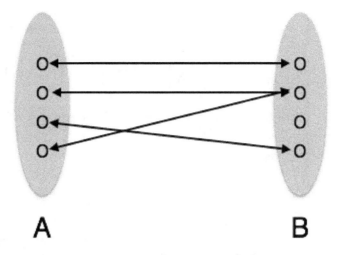

[Image: Many-to-one relation]

- **Many-to-many**: One entity from A can be associated with more than one entity from B and vice versa.

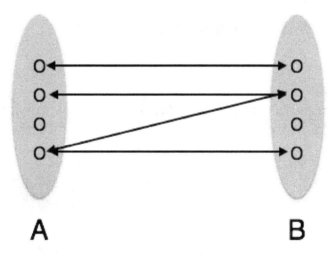

[Image: Many-to-many relation]

7. ER DIAGRAM REPRESENTATION

Let us now learn how the ER Model is represented by means of an ER diagram. Any object, for example, entities, attributes of an entity, relationship sets, and attributes of relationship sets, can be represented with the help of an ER diagram.

Entity

Entities are represented by means of rectangles. Rectangles are named with the entity set they represent.

Student	Teacher	Projects

[Image: Entities in a school database]

Attributes

Attributes are the properties of entities. Attributes are represented by means of ellipses. Every ellipse represents one attribute and is directly connected to its entity (rectangle).

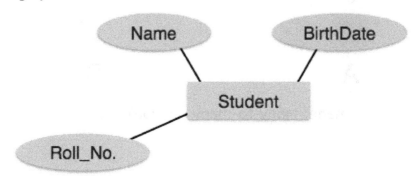

[Image: Simple Attributes]

If the attributes are **composite**, they are further divided in a tree like structure. Every node is then connected to its attribute. That is, composite attributes are represented by ellipses that are connected with an ellipse.

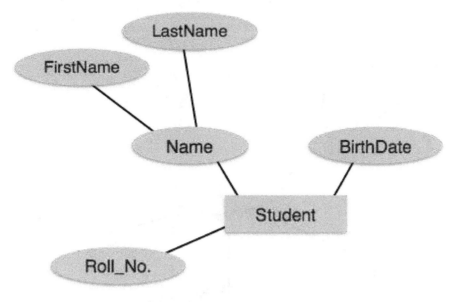

[*Image: Composite Attributes*]

Multivalued attributes are depicted by double ellipse.

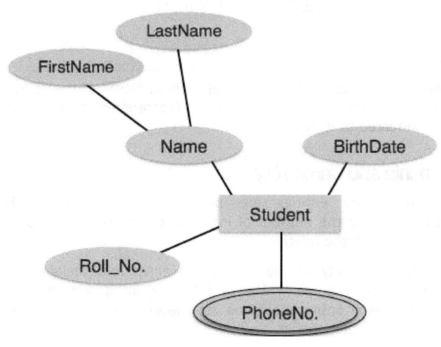

[*Image: Multivalued Attributes*]

Derived attributes are depicted by dashed ellipse.

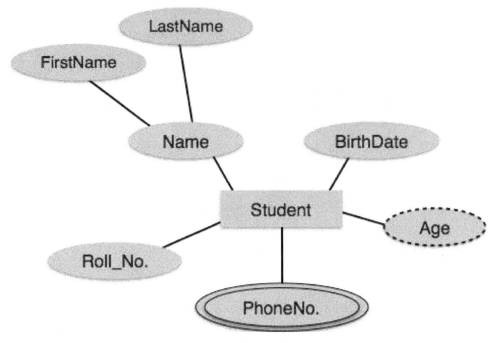

[*Image: Derived Attributes*]

Relationship

Relationships are represented by diamond-shaped box. Name of the relationship is written inside the diamond-box. All the entities (rectangles) participating in a relationship are connected to it by a line.

Binary Relationship and Cardinality

A relationship where two entities are participating is called a **binary relationship**. Cardinality is the number of instance of an entity from a relation that can be associated with the relation.

- **One-to-one:** When only one instance of an entity is associated with the relationship, it is marked as '1:1'. The following image reflects that only one instance of each entity should be associated with the relationship. It depicts one-to-one relationship.

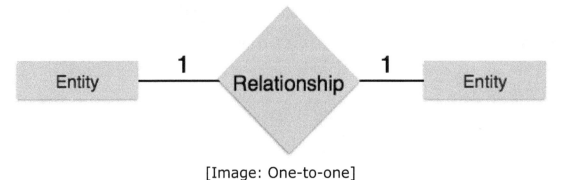

[Image: One-to-one]

- **One-to-many:** When more than one instance of an entity is associated with a relationship, it is marked as '1:N'. The following image reflects that only one instance of entity on the left and more than one instance of an entity on the right can be associated with the relationship. It depicts one-to-many relationship.

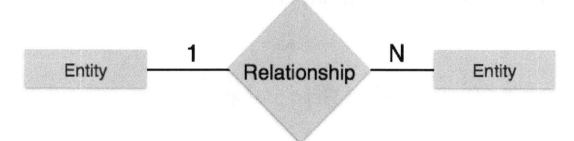

[Image: One-to-many]

- **Many-to-one:** When more than one instance of entity is associated with the relationship, it is marked as 'N:1'. The following image reflects that more than one instance of an entity on the left and only one instance of an entity on the right can be associated with the relationship. It depicts many-to-one relationship.

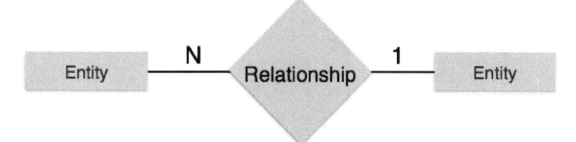

[Image: Many-to-one]

- **Many-to-many:** The following image reflects that more than one instance of an entity on the left and more than one instance of an entity on the right can be associated with the relationship. It depicts many-to-many relationship.

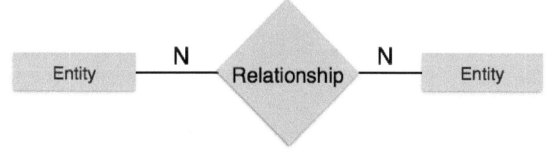

[Image: Many-to-many]

Participation Constraints

- **Total Participation**: Each entity is involved in the relationship. Total participation is represented by double lines.

- **Partial participation**: Not all entities are involved in the relationship. Partial participation is represented by single lines.

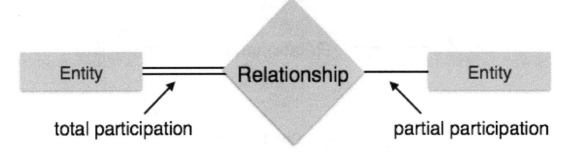

[Image: Participation Constraints]

8. GENERALIZATION & SPECIALIZATION

The ER Model has the power of expressing database entities in a conceptual hierarchical manner. As the hierarchy goes up, it generalizes the view of entities, and as we go deep in the hierarchy, it gives us the detail of every entity included.

Going up in this structure is called **generalization**, where entities are clubbed together to represent a more generalized view. For example, a particular student named Mira can be generalized along with all the students. The entity shall be a student, and further, the student is a person. The reverse is called **specialization** where a person is a student, and that student is Mira.

Generalization

As mentioned above, the process of generalizing entities, where the generalized entities contain the properties of all the generalized entities, is called generalization. In generalization, a number of entities are brought together into one generalized entity based on their similar characteristics. For example, pigeon, house sparrow, crow, and dove can all be generalized as Birds.

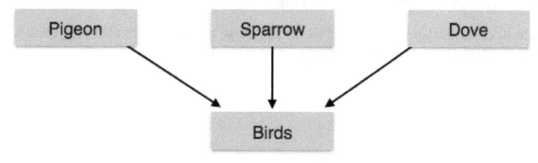

[*Image: Generalization*]

Specialization

Specialization is the opposite of generalization. In specialization, a group of entities is divided into sub-groups based on their characteristics. Take a group 'Person' for example. A person has name, date of birth, gender, etc. These properties are common in all persons, human beings. But in a company, persons can be identified as employee, employer, customer, or vendor, based on what role they play in the company.

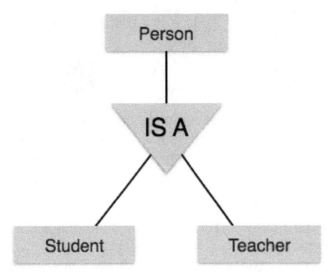

[*Image: Specialization*]

Similarly, in a school database, persons can be specialized as teacher, student, or a staff, based on what role they play in school as entities.

Inheritance

We use all the above features of ER-Model in order to create classes of objects in object-oriented programming. The details of entities are generally hidden from the user; this process known as **abstraction**.

Inheritance is an important feature of Generalization and Specialization. It allows lower-level entities to inherit the attributes of higher-level entities.

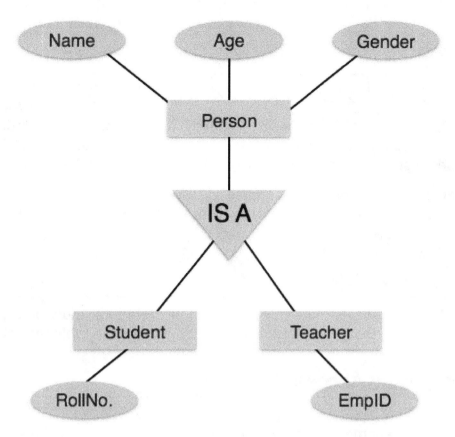

[Image: Inheritance]

For example, the attributes of a Person class such as name, age, and gender can be inherited by lower-level entities such as Student or Teacher.

9. CODD'S 12 RULES

Dr Edgar F. Codd, after his extensive research on the Relational Model of database systems, came up with twelve rules of his own, which according to him, a database must obey in order to be regarded as a true relational database.

These rules can be applied on any database system that manages stored data using only its relational capabilities. This is a foundation rule, which acts as a base for all the other rules.

Rule 1: Information Rule

The data stored in a database, may it be user data or metadata, must be a value of some table cell. Everything in a database must be stored in a table format.

Rule 2: Guaranteed Access Rule

Every single data element (value) is guaranteed to be accessible logically with a combination of table-name, primary-key (row value), and attribute-name (column value). No other means, such as pointers, can be used to access data.

Rule 3: Systematic Treatment of NULL Values

The NULL values in a database must be given a systematic and uniform treatment. This is a very important rule because a NULL can be interpreted as one the following: data is missing, data is not known, or data is not applicable.

Rule 4: Active Online Catalog

The structure description of the entire database must be stored in an online catalog, known as **data dictionary**, which can be accessed by authorized users. Users can use the same query language to access the catalog which they use to access the database itself.

Rule 5: Comprehensive Data Sub-Language Rule

A database can only be accessed using a language having linear syntax that supports data definition, data manipulation, and transaction management operations. This language can be used directly or by means of some application. If the database allows access to data without any help of this language, then it is considered as a violation.

Rule 6: View Updating Rule

All the views of a database, which can theoretically be updated, must also be updatable by the system.

Rule 7: High-Level Insert, Update, and Delete Rule

A database must support high-level insertion, updation, and deletion. This must not be limited to a single row, that is, it must also support union, intersection and minus operations to yield sets of data records.

Rule 8: Physical Data Independence

The data stored in a database must be independent of the applications that access the database. Any change in the physical structure of a database must not have any impact on how the data is being accessed by external applications.

Rule 9: Logical Data Independence

The logical data in a database must be independent of its user's view (application). Any change in logical data must not affect the applications using it. For example, if two tables are merged or one is split into two different tables, there should be no impact or change on the user application. This is one of the most difficult rule to apply.

Rule 10: Integrity Independence

A database must be independent of the application that uses it. All its integrity constraints can be independently modified without the need of any change in the application. This rule makes a database independent of the front-end application and its interface.

Rule 11: Distribution Independence

The end-user must not be able to see that the data is distributed over various locations. Users should always get the impression that the data is located at one site only. This rule has been regarded as the foundation of distributed database systems.

Rule 12: Non-Subversion Rule

If a system has an interface that provides access to low-level records, then the interface must not be able to subvert the system and bypass security and integrity constraints.

10. RELATIONAL DATA MODEL

Relational data model is the primary data model, which is used widely around the world for data storage and processing. This model is simple and it has all the properties and capabilities required to process data with storage efficiency.

Concepts

Tables: In relational data model, relations are saved in the format of Tables. This format stores the relation among entities. A table has rows and columns, where rows represent records and columns represent the attributes.

Tuple: A single row of a table, which contains a single record for that relation is called a tuple.

Relation instance: A finite set of tuples in the relational database system represents relation instance. Relation instances do not have duplicate tuples.

Relation schema: A relation schema describes the relation name (table name), attributes, and their names.

Relation key: Each row has one or more attributes, known as relation key, which can identify the row in the relation (table) uniquely.

Attribute domain: Every attribute has some predefined value scope, known as attribute domain.

Constraints

Every relation has some conditions that must hold for it to be a valid relation. These conditions are called **Relational Integrity Constraints**. There are three main integrity constraints:

- Key constraints
- Domain constraints
- Referential integrity constraints

Key Constraints

There must be at least one minimal subset of attributes in the relation, which can identify a tuple uniquely. This minimal subset of attributes is called **key** for that relation. If there are more than one such minimal subsets, these are called **candidate keys**.

Key constraints force that:

- in a relation with a key attribute, no two tuples can have identical values for key attributes.

- a key attribute cannot have NULL values.

Key constraints are also referred to as **Entity Constraints**.

Domain Constraints

Attributes have specific values in real-world scenario. For example, age can only be a positive integer. The same constraints have been tried to employ on the attributes of a relation. Every attribute is bound to have a specific range of values. For example, age cannot be less than zero and telephone numbers cannot contain a digit outside 0-9.

Referential Integrity Constraints

Referential integrity constraints work on the concept of Foreign Keys. A foreign key is a key attribute of a relation that can be referred in other relation.

Referential integrity constraint states that if a relation refers to a key attribute of a different or same relation, then that key element must exist.

11. RELATIONAL ALGEBRA

Relational database systems are expected to be equipped with a query language that can assist its users to query the database instances. There are two kinds of query languages: relational algebra and relational calculus.

Relational Algebra

Relational algebra is a procedural query language, which takes instances of relations as input and yields instances of relations as output. It uses operators to perform queries. An operator can be either **unary** or **binary**. They accept relations as their input and yield relations as their output. Relational algebra is performed recursively on a relation and intermediate results are also considered relations.

The fundamental operations of relational algebra are as follows:

- Select
- Project
- Union
- Set different
- Cartesian product
- Rename

We will discuss all these operations in the following sections.

Select Operation (σ)

It selects tuples that satisfy the given predicate from a relation.

Notation: $\sigma_p(r)$

Where **σ** stands for selection predicate and **r** stands for relation. *p* is prepositional logic formula which may use connectors like **and**, **or**, and **not**. These terms may use relational operators like: $=, \neq, \geq, <, >, \leq$.

For example:

$$\sigma_{subject="database"}(Books)$$

Output: Selects tuples from books where subject is 'database'.

$$\sigma_{subject="database" \text{ and } price="450"}(Books)$$

Output: Selects tuples from books where subject is 'database' and 'price' is 450.

$$\sigma_{subject="database"\ and\ price\ <\ "450"\ or\ year\ >\ "2010"}(Books)$$

Output: Selects tuples from books where subject is 'database' and 'price' is 450 or those books published after 2010.

Project Operation (∏)

It projects column(s) that satisfy a given predicate.

Notation: $\Pi_{A1,\ A2,\ An}(r)$

Where A_1, A_2, A_n are attribute names of relation **r**.

Duplicate rows are automatically eliminated, as relation is a set.

For example:

$$\Pi_{subject,\ author}(Books)$$

Selects and projects columns named as subject and author from the relation Books.

Union Operation (∪)

It performs binary union between two given relations and is defined as:

$$r\ ∪\ s = \{\ t\ |\ t ∈ r\ or\ t ∈ s\}$$

Notion: r ∪ s

Where **r** and **s** are either database relations or relation result set (temporary relation).

For a union operation to be valid, the following conditions must hold:

- **r** and **s** must have the same number of attributes.
- Attribute domains must be compatible.
- Duplicate tuples are automatically eliminated.

$$\Pi_{author}(Books)\ ∪\ \Pi_{author}(Articles)$$

Output: Projects the names of the authors who have either written a book or an article or both.

Set Difference (−)

The result of set difference operation is tuples, which are present in one relation but are not in the second relation.

Notation: **r − s**

Finds all the tuples that are present in **r** but not in **s**.

$$\prod_{author}(Books) - \prod_{author}(Articles)$$

Output: Provides the name of authors who have written books but not articles.

Cartesian Product (X)

Combines information of two different relations into one.

Notation: r X s

Where **r** and **s** are relations and their output will be defined as:

r X s = { q t | q ∈ r and t ∈ s}

$$\prod_{author = \text{'tutorialspoint'}}(Books \ X \ Articles)$$

Output: Yields a relation, which shows all the books and articles written by tutorialspoint.

Rename Operation (ρ)

The results of relational algebra are also relations but without any name. The rename operation allows us to rename the output relation. 'rename' operation is denoted with small Greek letter **rho** ρ.

Notation: $\rho_x(E)$

Where the result of expression **E** is saved with name of **x**.

Additional operations are:

- Set intersection
- Assignment
- Natural join

Relational Calculus

In contrast to Relational Algebra, Relational Calculus is a non-procedural query language, that is, it tells what to do but never explains how to do it.

Relational calculus exists in two forms:

Tuple Relational Calculus (TRC)

Filtering variable ranges over tuples

Notation: {T | Condition}

Returns all tuples T that satisfies a condition.

For example:

```
{ T.name |   Author(T) AND T.article = 'database' }
```

Output: Returns tuples with 'name' from Author who has written article on 'database'.

TRC can be quantified. We can use Existential (∃) and Universal Quantifiers (∀).

For example:

```
{ R| ∃T   ∈ Authors(T.article='database' AND R.name=T.name)}
```

Output: The above query will yield the same result as the previous one.

Domain Relational Calculus (DRC)

In DRC, the filtering variable uses the domain of attributes instead of entire tuple values (as done in TRC, mentioned above).

Notation:

$\{ a_1, a_2, a_3, ..., a_n \mid P (a_1, a_2, a_3, ... ,a_n)\}$

Where a_1, a_2 are attributes and **P** stands for formulae built by inner attributes.

For example:

```
{< article, page, subject > |   ∈ TutorialsPoint ∧ subject = 'database'}
```

Output: Yields Article, Page, and Subject from the relation TutorialsPoint, where subject is database.

Just like TRC, DRC can also be written using existential and universal quantifiers. DRC also involves relational operators.

The expression power of Tuple Relation Calculus and Domain Relation Calculus is equivalent to Relational Algebra.

12. ER MODEL TO RELATIONAL MODEL

ER Model, when conceptualized into diagrams, gives a good overview of entity-relationship, which is easier to understand. ER diagrams can be mapped to relational schema, that is, it is possible to create relational schema using ER diagram. We cannot import all the ER constraints into relational model, but an approximate schema can be generated.

There are several processes and algorithms available to convert ER Diagrams into Relational Schema. Some of them are automated and some of them are manual. We may focus here on the mapping diagram contents to relational basics.

ER diagrams mainly comprise of:

- Entity and its attributes

- Relationship, which is association among entities

Mapping Entity

An entity is a real-world object with some attributes.

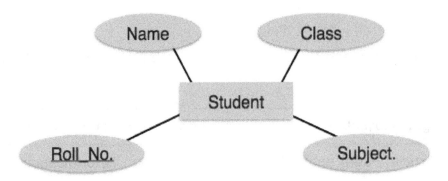

[*Image: Mapping Entity*]

Mapping Process (Algorithm)

- Create table for each entity.

- Entity's attributes should become fields of tables with their respective data types.

- Declare primary key.

Mapping Relationship

A relationship is an association among entities.

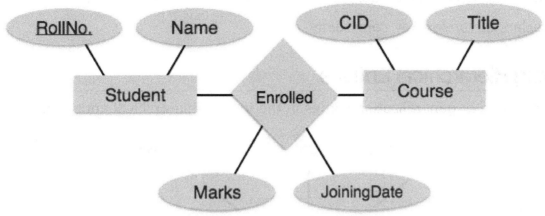

[*Image: Mapping relationship*]

Mapping Process:

- Create table for a relationship.

- Add the primary keys of all participating Entities as fields of table with their respective data types.

- If relationship has any attribute, add each attribute as field of table.

- Declare a primary key composing all the primary keys of participating entities.

- Declare all foreign key constraints.

Mapping Weak Entity Sets

A weak entity set is one which does not have any primary key associated with it.

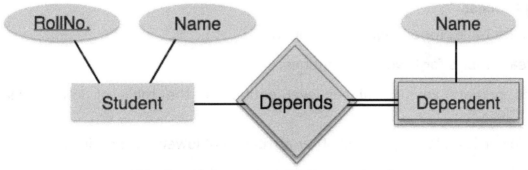

[*Image: Mapping Weak Entity Sets*]

Mapping Process:

- Create table for weak entity set.

- Add all its attributes to table as field.

- Add the primary key of identifying entity set.

- Declare all foreign key constraints.

Mapping Hierarchical Entities

ER specialization or generalization comes in the form of hierarchical entity sets.

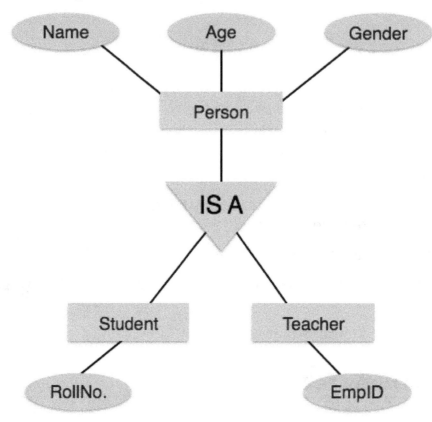

[*Image: Mapping hierarchical entities*]

Mapping Process

- Create tables for all higher-level entities.

- Create tables for lower-level entities.

- Add primary keys of higher-level entities in the table of lower-level entities.

- In lower-level tables, add all other attributes of lower-level entities.

- Declare primary key of higher-level table and the primary key for lower-level table.

- Declare foreign key constraints.

13. SQL OVERVIEW

SQL is a programming language for Relational Databases. It is designed over relational algebra and tuple relational calculus. SQL comes as a package with all major distributions of RDBMS.

SQL comprises both data definition and data manipulation languages. Using the data definition properties of SQL, one can design and modify database schema, whereas data manipulation properties allows SQL to store and retrieve data from database.

Data Definition Language

SQL uses the following set of commands to define database schema:

CREATE

Creates new databases, tables, and views from RDBMS.

For example:

```
Create database tutorialspoint;

Create table article;

Create view for_students;
```

DROP

Drops commands, views, tables, and databases from RDBMS.

For example:

```
Drop object_type object_name;

Drop database tutorialspoint;

Drop table article;

Drop view for_students;
```

ALTER

Modifies database schema.

```
Alter object_type object_name parameters;
```

For example:

```
Alter table article add subject varchar;
```

This command adds an attribute in the relation **article** with the name **subject** of string type.

Data Manipulation Language

SQL is equipped with data manipulation language (DML). DML modifies the database instance by inserting, updating, and deleting its data. DML is responsible for all forms data modification in a database. SQL contains the following set of commands in its DML section:

- SELECT/FROM/WHERE
- INSERT INTO/VALUES
- UPDATE/SET/WHERE
- DELETE FROM/WHERE

These basic constructs allow database programmers and users to enter data and information into the database and retrieve efficiently using a number of filter options.

SELECT/FROM/WHERE

- **SELECT**

   This is one of the fundamental query command of SQL. It is similar to the projection operation of relational algebra. It selects the attributes based on the condition described by WHERE clause.

- **FROM**

   This clause takes a relation name as an argument from which attributes are to be selected/projected. In case more than one relation names are given, this clause corresponds to Cartesian product.

- **WHERE**

   This clause defines predicate or conditions, which must match in order to qualify the attributes to be projected.

For example:

```
Select author_name
From book_author
Where age > 50;
```

This command will yield the names of authors from the relation **book_author** whose age is greater than 50.

INSERT INTO/VALUES

This command is used for inserting values into the rows of a table (relation).

Syntax:

```
INSERT INTO table (column1 [, column2, column3 ... ]) VALUES (value1 [,
value2, value3 ... ])
```

Or

```
INSERT INTO table VALUES (value1, [value2, ... ])
```

For example:

```
INSERT INTO tutorialspoint (Author, Subject) VALUES ("anonymous",
"computers");
```

UPDATE/SET/WHERE

This command is used for updating or modifying the values of columns in a table (relation).

Syntax:

```
UPDATE table_name SET column_name = value [, column_name = value ...]
[WHERE condition]
```

For example:

```
UPDATE tutorialspoint SET Author="webmaster" WHERE Author="anonymous";
```

DELETE/FROM/WHERE

This command is used for removing one or more rows from a table (relation).

Syntax:

```
DELETE FROM table_name [WHERE condition];
```

For example:

```
DELETE FROM tutorialspoint
   WHERE Author="unknown";
```

14. NORMALIZATION

Functional Dependency

Functional dependency (FD) is a set of constraints between two attributes in a relation. Functional dependency says that if two tuples have same values for attributes A_1, A_2,..., A_n, then those two tuples must have to have same values for attributes B_1, B_2, ..., B_n.

Functional dependency is represented by an arrow sign ($\rightarrow$) that is, X$\rightarrow$Y, where X functionally determines Y. The left-hand side attributes determine the values of attributes on the right-hand side.

Armstrong's Axioms

If F is a set of functional dependencies then the closure of F, denoted as F^+, is the set of all functional dependencies logically implied by F. Armstrong's Axioms are a set of rules that, when applied repeatedly, generates a closure of functional dependencies.

- **Reflexive rule**: If alpha is a set of attributes and beta is_subset_of alpha, then alpha holds beta.

- **Augmentation rule**: If a $\rightarrow$ b holds and y is attribute set, then ay $\rightarrow$ by also holds. That is adding attributes in dependencies, does not change the basic dependencies.

- **Transitivity rule**: Same as transitive rule in algebra, if a $\rightarrow$ b holds and b $\rightarrow$ c holds, then a $\rightarrow$ c also holds. a $\rightarrow$ b is called as a functionally that determines b.

Trivial Functional Dependency

- **Trivial**: If a functional dependency (FD) X $\rightarrow$ Y holds, where Y is a subset of X, then it is called a trivial FD. Trivial FDs always hold.

- **Non-trivial**: If an FD X $\rightarrow$ Y holds, where Y is not a subset of X, then it is called a non-trivial FD.

- **Completely non-trivial**: If an FD X $\rightarrow$ Y holds, where x intersect Y = Φ, it is said to be a completely non-trivial FD.

Normalization

If a database design is not perfect, it may contain anomalies, which are like a bad dream for any database administrator. Managing a database with anomalies is next to impossible.

- **Update anomalies**: If data items are scattered and are not linked to each other properly, then it could lead to strange situations. For example, when we try to update one data item having its copies scattered over several places, a few instances get updated properly while a few others are left with old values. Such instances leave the database in an inconsistent state.

- **Deletion anomalies**: We tried to delete a record, but parts of it was left undeleted because of unawareness, the data is also saved somewhere else.

- **Insert anomalies**: We tried to insert data in a record that does not exist at all.

Normalization is a method to remove all these anomalies and bring the database to a consistent state.

First Normal Form

First Normal Form is defined in the definition of relations (tables) itself. This rule defines that all the attributes in a relation must have atomic domains. The values in an atomic domain are indivisible units.

Course	Content
Programming	Java, c++
Web	HTML, PHP, ASP

[Image: Unorganized relation]

We re-arrange the relation (table) as below, to convert it to First Normal Form.

Course	Content
Programming	Java
Programming	c++
Web	HTML
Web	PHP
Web	ASP

[Image: Relation in 1NF]

Each attribute must contain only a single value from its predefined domain.

Second Normal Form

Before we learn about the second normal form, we need to understand the following:

- **Prime attribute**: An attribute, which is a part of the prime-key, is known as a prime attribute.

- **Non-prime attribute**: An attribute, which is not a part of the prime-key, is said to be a non-prime attribute.

If we follow second normal form, then every non-prime attribute should be fully functionally dependent on prime key attribute. That is, if X → A holds, then there should not be any proper subset Y of X for which Y → A also holds true.

Student_Project

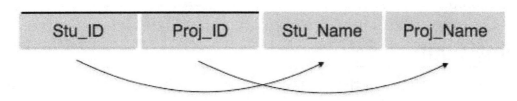

[Image: Relation not in 2NF]

We see here in Student_Project relation that the prime key attributes are Stu_ID and Proj_ID. According to the rule, non-key attributes, i.e., Stu_Name and Proj_Name must be dependent upon both and not on any of the prime key attribute individually. But we find that Stu_Name can be identified by Stu_ID and Proj_Name can be identified by Proj_ID independently. This is called **partial dependency**, which is not allowed in Second Normal Form.

Student

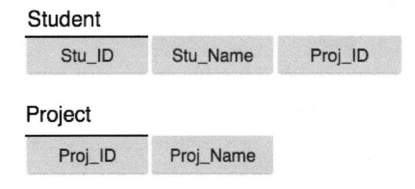

Project

[Image: Relation in 2NF]

We broke the relation in two as depicted in the above picture. So there exists no partial dependency.

Third Normal Form

For a relation to be in Third Normal Form, it must be in Second Normal form and the following must satisfy:

- No non-prime attribute is transitively dependent on prime key attribute.

- For any non-trivial functional dependency, $X \rightarrow A$, then either:

    o X is a superkey or,

    o A is prime attribute.

Student_Detail

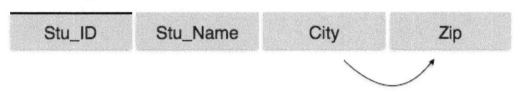

[Image: Relation not in 3NF]

We find that in the above Student_detail relation, Stu_ID is the key and only prime key attribute. We find that City can be identified by Stu_ID as well as Zip itself. Neither Zip is a superkey nor is City a prime attribute. Additionally, Stu_ID $\rightarrow$ Zip $\rightarrow$ City, so there exists **transitive dependency**.

To bring this relation into third normal form, we break the relation into two relations as follows:

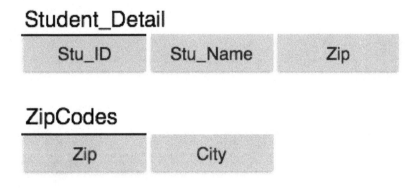

[Image: Relation in 3NF]

Boyce-Codd Normal Form

Boyce-Codd Normal Form (BCNF) is an extension of Third Normal Form on strict terms. BCNF states that -

- For any non-trivial functional dependency, X → A, X must be a super-key.

In the above image, Stu_ID is the super-key in the relation Student_Detail and Zip is the super-key in the relation ZipCodes. So,

> Stu_ID → Stu_Name, Zip

and

> Zip → City

Which confirms that both the relations are in BCNF.

15. JOINS

We understand the benefits of taking a Cartesian product of two relations, which gives us all the possible tuples that are paired together. But it might not be feasible for us in certain cases to take a Cartesian product where we encounter huge relations with thousands of tuples having a considerable large number of attributes.

Join is a combination of a Cartesian product followed by a selection process. A Join operation pairs two tuples from different relations, if and only if a given join condition is satisfied.

We will briefly describe various join types in the following sections.

Theta (θ) Join

Theta join combines tuples from different relations provided they satisfy the theta condition. The join condition is denoted by the symbol **θ**.

Notation:

```
R1 ⋈θ R2
```

R1 and R2 are relations having attributes (A_1, A_2, .., A_n) and (B_1, B_2,.. ,B_n) such that the attributes don't have anything in common, that is, R1 ∩ R2 = Φ.

Theta join can use all kinds of comparison operators.

Student		
SID	**Name**	**Std**
101	Alex	10
102	Maria	11

[Table: Student Relation]

Subjects	
Class	Subject
10	Math
10	English
11	Music
11	Sports

[Table: Subjects Relation]

Student_Detail = STUDENT $\bowtie$Student.Std = Subject.Class **SUBJECT**

Student_detail				
SID	Name	Std	Class	Subject
101	Alex	10	10	Math
101	Alex	10	10	English
102	Maria	11	11	Music
102	Maria	11	11	Sports

[Table: Output of theta join]

Equijoin

When Theta join uses only **equality** comparison operator, it is said to be equijoin. The above example corresponds to equijoin.

Natural Join (⋈)

Natural join does not use any comparison operator. It does not concatenate the way a Cartesian product does. We can perform a Natural Join only if there is at least one common attribute that exists between two relations. In addition, the attributes must have the same name and domain.

Natural join acts on those matching attributes where the values of attributes in both the relations are same.

Courses		
CID	**Course**	**Dept**
CS01	Database	CS
ME01	Mechanics	ME
EE01	Electronics	EE

[Table: Relation Courses]

HoD	
Dept	**Head**
CS	Alex
ME	Maya
EE	Mira

[Table: Relation HoD]

Courses ⋈ HoD			
Dept	**CID**	**Course**	**Head**
CS	CS01	Database	Alex
ME	ME01	Mechanics	Maya
EE	EE01	Electronics	Mira

[Table: Relation Courses ⋈ HoD]

Outer Joins

Theta Join, Equijoin, and Natural Join are called inner joins. An inner join includes only those tuples with matching attributes and the rest are discarded in the resulting relation. Therefore, we need to use outer joins to include all the tuples from the participating relations in the resulting relation. There are three kinds of outer joins: left outer join, right outer join, and full outer join.

Left Outer Join (R ⟕ S)

All the tuples from the Left relation, R, are included in the resulting relation. If there are tuples in R without any matching tuple in the Right relation S, then the S-attributes of the resulting relation are made NULL.

Left	
A	**B**
100	Database
101	Mechanics
102	Electronics

[Table: Left Relation]

Right	
A	**B**
100	Alex
102	Maya
104	Mira

[Table: Right Relation]

Courses	HoD		
A	B	C	D
100	Database	100	Alex
101	Mechanics	---	---
102	Electronics	102	Maya

[Table: Left outer join output]

Right Outer Join: (R ⋈ S)

All the tuples from the Right relation, S, are included in the resulting relation. If there are tuples in S without any matching tuple in R, then the R-attributes of resulting relation are made NULL.

Courses	HoD		
A	B	C	D
100	Database	100	Alex
102	Electronics	102	Maya
---	---	104	Mira

[Table: Right outer join output]

Full Outer Join: (R ⋈ S)

All the tuples from both participating relations are included in the resulting relation. If there are no matching tuples for both relations, their respective unmatched attributes are made NULL.

	Courses	HoD	
A	B	C	D
100	Database	100	Alex
101	Mechanics	---	---
102	Electronics	102	Maya
---	---	104	Mira

[Table: Full outer join output]

16. STORAGE SYSTEM

Databases are stored in file formats, which contain records. At physical level, the actual data is stored in electromagnetic format on some device. These storage devices can be broadly categorized into three types:

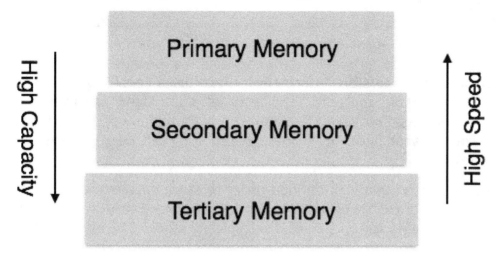

[*Image: Memory Types*]

- **Primary Storage**: The memory storage that is directly accessible to the CPU comes under this category. CPU's internal memory (registers), fast memory (cache), and main memory (RAM) are directly accessible to the CPU, as they are all placed on the motherboard or CPU chipset. This storage is typically very small, ultra-fast, and volatile. Primary storage requires continuous power supply in order to maintain its state. In case of a power failure, all its data is lost.

- **Secondary Storage**: Secondary storage devices are used to store data for future use or as backup. Secondary storage includes memory devices that are not a part of the CPU chipset or motherboard, for example, magnetic disks, optical disks (DVD, CD, etc.), hard disks, flash drives, and magnetic tapes.

- **Tertiary Storage**: Tertiary storage is used to store huge volumes of data. Since such storage devices are external to the computer system, they are the slowest in speed. These storage devices are mostly used to take the back up of an entire system. Optical disks and magnetic tapes are widely used as tertiary storage.

Memory Hierarchy

A computer system has a well-defined hierarchy of memory. A CPU has direct access to it main memory as well as its inbuilt registers. The access time of the main memory is obviously less than the CPU speed. To minimize this speed mismatch, cache memory is introduced. Cache memory provides the fastest access time and it contains data that is most frequently accessed by the CPU.

The memory with the fastest access is the costliest one. Larger storage devices offer slow speed and they are less expensive, however they can store huge volumes of data as compared to CPU registers or cache memory.

Magnetic Disks

Hard disk drives are the most common secondary storage devices in present computer systems. These are called magnetic disks because they use the concept of magnetization to store information. Hard disks consist of metal disks coated with magnetizable material. These disks are placed vertically on a spindle. A read/write head moves in between the disks and is used to magnetize or de-magnetize the spot under it. A magnetized spot can be recognized as 0 (zero) or 1 (one).

Hard disks are formatted in a well-defined order to store data efficiently. A hard disk plate has many concentric circles on it, called **tracks**. Every track is further divided into **sectors**. A sector on a hard disk typically stores 512 bytes of data.

RAID

RAID stands for **R**edundant **A**rray of **I**ndependent **D**isks, which is a technology to connect multiple secondary storage devices and use them as a single storage media.

RAID consists of an array of disks in which multiple disks are connected together to achieve different goals. RAID levels define the use of disk arrays.

- **RAID 0**: In this level, a striped array of disks is implemented. The data is broken down into blocks and the blocks are distributed among disks. Each disk receives a block of data to write/read in parallel. It enhances the speed and performance of the storage device. There is no parity and backup in Level 0.

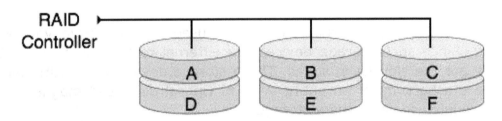

[Image: RAID 0]

- **RAID 1**: RAID 1 uses mirroring techniques. When data is sent to a RAID controller, it sends a copy of data to all the disks in the array. RAID level

1 is also called **mirroring** and provides 100% redundancy in case of a failure.

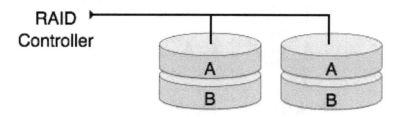

[Image: RAID 1]

- **RAID 2**: RAID 2 records Error Correction Code using Hamming distance for its data, striped on different disks. Like level 0, each data bit in a word is recorded on a separate disk and ECC codes of the data words are stored on a different set disks. Due to its complex structure and high cost, RAID 2 is not commercially available.

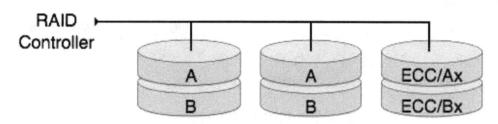

[Image: RAID 2]

- **RAID 3**: RAID 3 stripes the data onto multiple disks. The parity bit generated for data word is stored on a different disk. This technique makes it to overcome single disk failures.

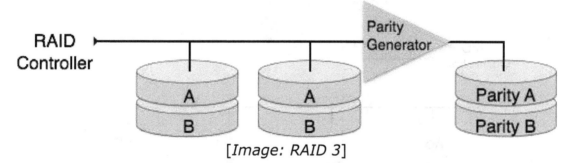

[Image: RAID 3]

- **RAID 4**: In this level, an entire block of data is written onto data disks and then the parity is generated and stored on a different disk. Note that level 3 uses byte-level striping, whereas level 4 uses block-level striping. Both level 3 and level 4 require at least three disks to implement RAID.

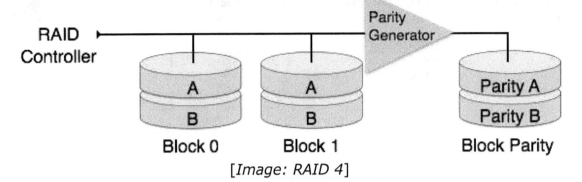

[*Image: RAID 4*]

- **RAID 5**: RAID 5 writes whole data blocks onto different disks, but the parity bits generated for data block stripe are distributed among all the data disks rather than storing them on a different dedicated disk.

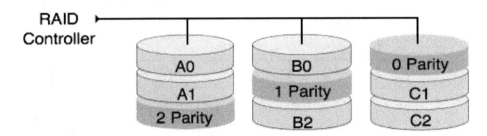

[Image: RAID 5]

- **RAID 6**: RAID 6 is an extension of level 5. In this level, two independent parities are generated and stored in distributed fashion among multiple disks. Two parities provide additional fault tolerance. This level requires at least four disk drives to implement RAID.

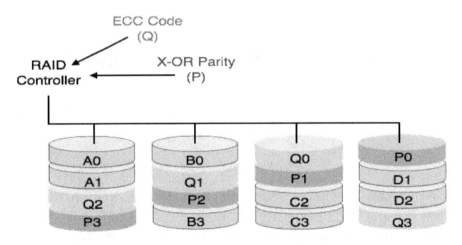

[Image: RAID 6]

17. FILE STRUCTURE

Relative data and information is stored collectively in file formats. A file is a sequence of records stored in binary format. A disk drive is formatted into several blocks that can store records. File records are mapped onto those disk blocks.

File Organization

File Organization defines how file records are mapped onto disk blocks. We have four types of File Organization to organize file records:

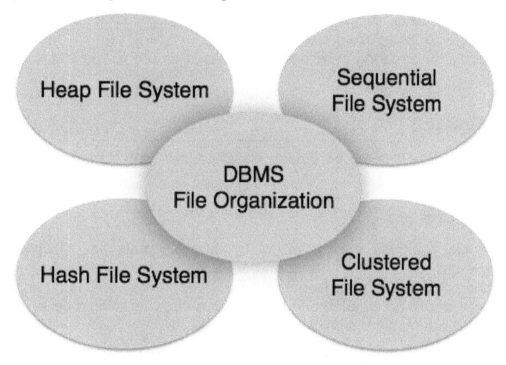

[*Image: File Organization*]

Heap File Organization

When a file is created using Heap File Organization, the Operating System allocates memory area to that file without any further accounting details. File records can be placed anywhere in that memory area. It is the responsibility of the software to manage the records. Heap File does not support any ordering, sequencing, or indexing on its own.

Sequential File Organization

Every file record contains a data field (attribute) to uniquely identify that record. In sequential file organization, records are placed in the file in some sequential order based on the unique key field or search key. Practically, it is not possible to store all the records sequentially in physical form.

Hash File Organization

Hash File Organization uses Hash function computation on some fields of the records. The output of the hash function determines the location of disk block where the records are to be placed.

Clustered File Organization

Clustered file organization is not considered good for large databases. In this mechanism, related records from one or more relations are kept in the same disk block, that is, the ordering of records is not based on primary key or search key.

File Operations

Operations on database files can be broadly classified into two categories:

- Update Operations
- Retrieval Operations

Update operations change the data values by insertion, deletion, or update. Retrieval operations, on the other hand, do not alter the data but retrieve them after optional conditional filtering. In both types of operations, selection plays a significant role. Other than creation and deletion of a file, there could be several operations, which can be done on files.

- **Open**: A file can be opened in one of the two modes, **read mode** or **write mode**. In read mode, the operating system does not allow anyone to alter data. In other words, data is read only. Files opened in read mode can be shared among several entities. Write mode allows data modification. Files opened in write mode can be read but cannot be shared.

- **Locate**: Every file has a file pointer, which tells the current position where the data is to be read or written. This pointer can be adjusted accordingly. Using find (seek) operation, it can be moved forward or backward.

- **Read**: By default, when files are opened in read mode, the file pointer points to the beginning of the file. There are options where the user can tell the operating system where to locate the file pointer at the time of opening a file. The very next data to the file pointer is read.

- **Write**: User can select to open a file in write mode, which enables them to edit its contents. It can be deletion, insertion, or modification. The file pointer can be located at the time of opening or can be dynamically changed if the operating system allows to do so.

- **Close**: This is the most important operation from the operating system's point of view. When a request to close a file is generated, the operating system

  o removes all the locks (if in shared mode),

  o saves the data (if altered) to the secondary storage media, and

  o releases all the buffers and file handlers associated with the file.

The organization of data inside a file plays a major role here. The process to locate the file pointer to a desired record inside a file various based on whether the records are arranged sequentially or clustered.

18. INDEXING

We know that data is stored in the form of records. Every record has a key field, which helps it to be recognized uniquely.

Indexing is a data structure technique to efficiently retrieve records from the database files based on some attributes on which the indexing has been done. Indexing in database systems is similar to what we see in books.

Indexing is defined based on its indexing attributes. Indexing can be of the following types:

- **Primary Index**: Primary index is defined on an ordered data file. The data file is ordered on a **key field**. The key field is generally the primary key of the relation.

- **Secondary Index**: Secondary index may be generated from a field which is a candidate key and has a unique value in every record, or a non-key with duplicate values.

- **Clustering Index**: Clustering index is defined on an ordered data file. The data file is ordered on a non-key field.

Ordered Indexing is of two types:

- Dense Index

- Sparse Index

Dense Index

In dense index, there is an index record for every search key value in the database. This makes searching faster but requires more space to store index records itself. Index records contain search key value and a pointer to the actual record on the disk.

[Image: Dense Index]

Sparse Index

In sparse index, index records are not created for every search key. An index record here contains a search key and an actual pointer to the data on the disk. To search a record, we first proceed by index record and reach at the actual location of the data. If the data we are looking for is not where we directly reach by following the index, then the system starts sequential search until the desired data is found.

[Image: Sparse Index]

Multilevel Index

Index records comprise search-key values and data pointers. Multilevel index is stored on the disk along with the actual database files. As the size of the database grows, so does the size of the indices. There is an immense need to keep the index records in the main memory so as to speed up the search operations. If single-level index is used, then a large size index cannot be kept in memory which leads to multiple disk accesses.

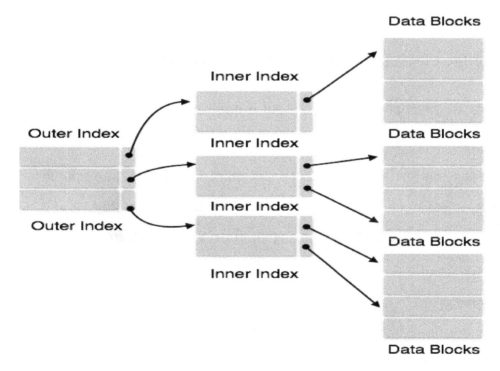

[Image: Multi-level Index]

Multi-level Index helps in breaking down the index into several smaller indices in order to make the outermost level so small that it can be saved in a single disk block, which can easily be accommodated anywhere in the main memory.

B⁺ Tree

A B⁺ tree is a balanced binary search tree that follows a multi-level index format. The leaf nodes of a B⁺ tree denote actual data pointers. B⁺ tree ensures that all leaf nodes remain at the same height, thus balanced. Additionally, the leaf nodes are linked using a link list; therefore, a B⁺ tree can support random access as well as sequential access.

Structure of B⁺ Tree

Every leaf node is at equal distance from the root node. A B⁺ tree is of the order **n** where **n** is fixed for every B⁺ tree.

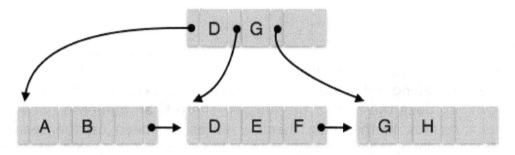

[*Image: B⁺ tree*]

Internal nodes:

- Internal (non-leaf) nodes contain at least [n/2] pointers, except the root node.

- At most, an internal node can contain **n** pointers.

Leaf nodes:

- Leaf nodes contain at least [n/2] record pointers and [n/2] key values.

- At most, a leaf node can contain **n** record pointers and **n** key values.

- Every leaf node contains one block pointer **P** to point to next leaf node and forms a linked list.

B⁺ Tree Insertion

- B⁺ trees are filled from bottom and each entry is done at the leaf node.

- If a leaf node overflows:

  o Split node into two parts.

- Partition at $i = \lfloor (m+1)_{/2} \rfloor$.

- First i entries are stored in one node.

- Rest of the entries (i+1 onwards) are moved to a new node.

- i^{th} key is duplicated at the parent of the leaf.

- If a non-leaf node overflows:

  - Split node into two parts.

  - Partition the node at $i = \lceil (m+1)_{/2} \rceil$.

  - Entries up to i are kept in one node.

  - Rest of the entries are moved to a new node.

B⁺ Tree Deletion

- B$^+$ tree entries are deleted at the leaf nodes.

- The target entry is searched and deleted.

  - If it is an internal node, delete and replace with the entry from the left position.

- After deletion, underflow is tested,

  - If underflow occurs, distribute the entries from the nodes left to it.

- If distribution is not possible from left, then

  - Distribute the entries from the nodes right to it.

- If distribution is not possible from left or from right, then

  - Merge the node with left and right to it.

19. HASHING

For a huge database structure, it can be almost next to impossible to search all the index values through all its level and then reach the destination data block to retrieve the desired data. Hashing is an effective technique to calculate the direct location of a data record on the disk without using index structure.

Hashing uses hash functions with search keys as parameters to generate the address of a data record.

Hash Organization

- **Bucket**: A hash file stores data in bucket format. Bucket is considered a unit of storage. A bucket typically stores one complete disk block, which in turn can store one or more records.

- **Hash Function**: A hash function, **h**, is a mapping function that maps all the set of search-keys **K** to the address where actual records are placed. It is a function from search keys to bucket addresses.

Static Hashing

In static hashing, when a search-key value is provided, the hash function always computes the same address. For example, if mod-4 hash function is used, then it shall generate only 5 values. The output address shall always be same for that function. The number of buckets provided remains unchanged at all times.

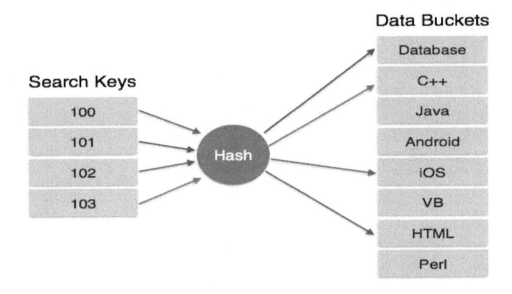

[Image: Static Hashing]

Operation:

- **Insertion**: When a record is required to be entered using static hash, the hash function **h** computes the bucket address for search key **K**, where the record will be stored.

  Bucket address = h(K)

- **Search**: When a record needs to be retrieved, the same hash function can be used to retrieve the address of the bucket where the data is stored.

- **Delete**: This is simply a search followed by a deletion operation.

Bucket Overflow

The condition of bucket-overflow is known as **collision**. This is a fatal state for any static hash function. In this case, overflow chaining can be used.

- **Overflow Chaining**: When buckets are full, a new bucket is allocated for the same hash result and is linked after the previous one. This mechanism is called **Closed Hashing**.

Data Buckets

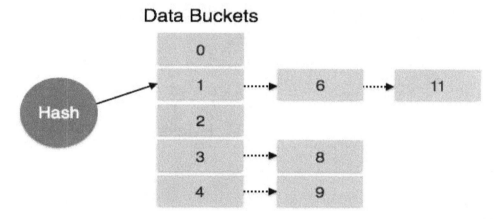

[Image: Overflow chaining]

- **Linear Probing**: When a hash function generates an address at which data is already stored, the next free bucket is allocated to it. This mechanism is called **Open Hashing**.

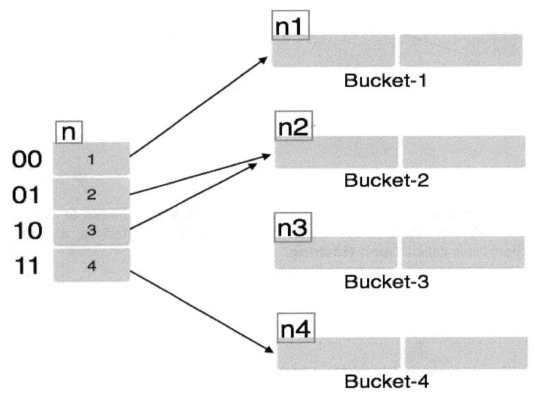

[Image: Linear Probing]

Dynamic Hashing

The problem with static hashing is that it does not expand or shrink dynamically as the size of the database grows or shrinks. Dynamic hashing provides a mechanism in which data buckets are added and removed dynamically and on-demand. Dynamic hashing is also known as **extended hashing**.

Hash function, in dynamic hashing, is made to produce a large number of values and only a few are used initially.

[Image: Dynamic Hashing]

Organization

The prefix of an entire hash value is taken as a hash index. Only a portion of the hash value is used for computing bucket addresses. Every hash index has a depth value to signify how many bits are used for computing a hash function. These bits can address 2n buckets. When all these bits are consumed — that is, when all the buckets are full — then the depth value is increased linearly and twice the buckets are allocated.

Operation

- **Querying**: Look at the depth value of the hash index and use those bits to compute the bucket address.

- **Update**: Perform a query as above and update the data.

- **Deletion**: Perform a query to locate the desired data and delete the same.

- **Insertion**: Compute the address of the bucket.

  - If the bucket is already full,

    - Add more buckets.

    - Add additional bits to the hash value.

    - Re-compute the hash function.

  - Else,

    - Add data to the bucket,

  - If all the buckets are full, perform the remedies of static hashing.

Hashing is not favorable when the data is organized in some ordering and the queries require a range of data. When data is discrete and random, hash performs the best.

Hashing algorithms have high complexity than indexing. All hash operations are done in constant time.

20. TRANSACTION

A transaction can be defined as a group of tasks. A single task is the minimum processing unit which cannot be divided further.

Let's take an example of a simple transaction. Suppose a bank employee transfers Rs 500 from A's account to B's account. This very simple and small transaction involves several low-level tasks.

A's Account

```
Open_Account(A)
Old_Balance = A.balance
New_Balance = Old_Balance - 500
A.balance = New_Balance
Close_Account(A)
```

B's Account

```
Open_Account(B)
Old_Balance = B.balance
New_Balance = Old_Balance + 500
B.balance = New_Balance
Close_Account(B)
```

ACID Properties

A transaction is a very small unit of a program and it may contain several low-level tasks. A transaction in a database system must maintain **A**tomicity, **C**onsistency, **I**solation, and **D**urability — commonly known as ACID properties — in order to ensure accuracy, completeness, and data integrity.

- **Atomicity**: This property states that a transaction must be treated as an atomic unit, that is, either all of its operations are executed or none. There must be no state in a database where a transaction is left partially completed. States should be defined either before the execution of the transaction or after the execution/abortion/failure of the transaction.

- **Consistency**: The database must remain in a consistent state after any transaction. No transaction should have any adverse effect on the data residing in the database. If the database was in a consistent state before the execution of a transaction, it must remain consistent after the execution of the transaction as well.

- **Durability**: The database should be durable enough to hold all its latest updates even if the system fails or restarts. If a transaction updates a chunk of data in a database and commits, then the database will hold the modified data. If a transaction commits but the system fails before the data could be written on to the disk, then that data will be updated once the system springs back into action.

- **Isolation**: In a database system where more than one transaction are being executed simultaneously and in parallel, the property of isolation states that all the transactions will be carried out and executed as if it is the only transaction in the system. No transaction will affect the existence of any other transaction.

Serializability

When multiple transactions are being executed by the operating system in a multiprogramming environment, there are possibilities that instructions of one transaction are interleaved with some other transaction.

- **Schedule**: A chronological execution sequence of a transaction is called a schedule. A schedule can have many transactions in it, each comprising of a number of instructions/tasks.

- **Serial Schedule**: It is a schedule in which transactions are aligned in such a way that one transaction is executed first. When the first transaction completes its cycle, then the next transaction is executed. Transactions are ordered one after the other. This type of schedule is called a serial schedule, as transactions are executed in a serial manner.

In a multi-transaction environment, serial schedules are considered as a benchmark. The execution sequence of an instruction in a transaction cannot be changed, but two transactions can have their instructions executed in a random fashion. This execution does no harm if two transactions are mutually independent and working on different segments of data; but in case these two transactions are working on the same data, then the results may vary. This ever-varying result may bring the database to an inconsistent state.

To resolve this problem, we allow parallel execution of a transaction schedule, if its transactions are either serializable or have some equivalence relation among them.

Equivalence Schedules

An equivalence schedule can be of the following types:

Result Equivalence

If two schedules produce the same result after execution, they are said to be result equivalent. They may yield the same result for some value and different results for another set of values. That's why this equivalence is not generally considered significant.

View Equivalence

Two schedules would be view equivalence if the transactions in both the schedules perform similar actions in a similar manner.

For example:

- If T reads the initial data in S1, then it also reads the initial data in S2.

- If T reads the value written by J in S1, then it also reads the value written by J in S2.

- If T performs the final write on the data value in S1, then it also performs the final write on the data value in S2.

Conflict Equivalence

Two schedules would be conflicting if they have the following properties:

- Both belong to separate transactions.

- Both accesses the same data item.

- At least one of them is "write" operation.

Two schedules having multiple transactions with conflicting operations are said to be conflict equivalent if and only if:

- Both the schedules contain the same set of Transactions.

- The order of conflicting pairs of operation is maintained in both the schedules.

Note: View equivalent schedules are view serializable and conflict equivalent schedules are conflict serializable. All conflict serializable schedules are view serializable too.

States of Transactions

A transaction in a database can be in one of the following states:

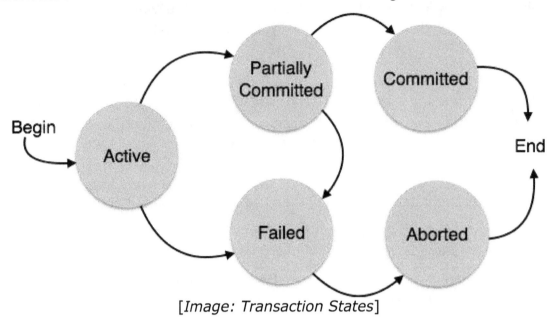

[*Image: Transaction States*]

- **Active**: In this state, the transaction is being executed. This is the initial state of every transaction.

- **Partially Committed**: When a transaction executes its final operation, it is said to be in a partially committed state.

- **Failed**: A transaction is said to be in a failed state if any of the checks made by the database recovery system fails. A failed transaction can no longer proceed further.

- **Aborted**: If any of the checks fails and the transaction has reached a failed state, then the recovery manager rolls back all its write operations on the database to bring the database back to its original state where it was prior to the execution of the transaction. Transactions in this state are called aborted. The database recovery module can select one of the two operations after a transaction aborts:

  o Re-start the transaction

  o Kill the transaction

- **Committed**: If a transaction executes all its operations successfully, it is said to be committed. All its effects are now permanently established on the database system.

21. CONCURRENCY CONTROL

In a multiprogramming environment where multiple transactions can be executed simultaneously, it is highly important to control the concurrency of transactions. We have concurrency control protocols to ensure atomicity, isolation, and serializability of concurrent transactions. Concurrency control protocols can be broadly divided into two categories:

- Lock-based protocols

- Timestamp-based protocols

Lock-based Protocols

Database systems equipped with lock-based protocols use a mechanism by which any transaction cannot read or write data until it acquires an appropriate lock on it. Locks are of two kinds:

- **Binary Locks**   A lock on a data item can be in two states; it is either locked or unlocked.

- **Shared/exclusive Locks** This type of locking mechanism differentiates the locks based on their uses. If a lock is acquired on a data item to perform a write operation, it is an exclusive lock. Allowing more than one transaction to write on the same data item would lead the database into an inconsistent state. Read locks are shared because no data value is being changed.

There are four types of lock protocols available:

Simplistic Lock Protocol

Simplistic lock-based protocols allow transactions to obtain a lock on every object before a 'write' operation is performed. Transactions may unlock the data item after completing the 'write' operation.

Pre-claiming Lock Protocol

Pre-claiming protocols evaluate their operations and create a list of data items on which they need locks. Before initiating an execution, the transaction requests the system for all the locks it needs beforehand. If all the locks are granted, the transaction executes and releases all the locks when all its operations are over. If all the locks are not granted, the transaction rolls back and waits until all the locks are granted.

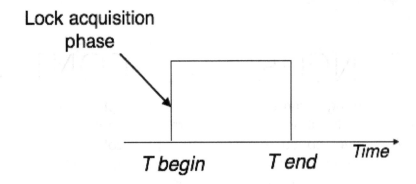

[Image: Pre-claiming]

Two-Phase Locking – 2PL

This locking protocol divides the execution phase of a transaction into three parts. In the first part, when the transaction starts executing, it seeks permission for the locks it requires. The second part is where the transaction acquires all the locks. As soon as the transaction releases its first lock, the third phase starts. In this phase, the transaction cannot demand any new locks; it only releases the acquired locks.

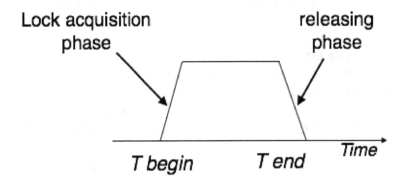

[Image: Two Phase Locking]

Two-phase locking has two phases, one is **growing**, where all the locks are being acquired by the transaction; and the second phase is shrinking, where the locks held by the transaction are being released.

To claim an exclusive (write) lock, a transaction must first acquire a shared (read) lock and then upgrade it to an exclusive lock.

Strict Two-Phase Locking

The first phase of Strict-2PL is same as 2PL. After acquiring all the locks in the first phase, the transaction continues to execute normally. But in contrast to 2PL, Strict-2PL does not release a lock after using it. Strict-2PL holds all the locks until the commit point and releases all the locks at a time.

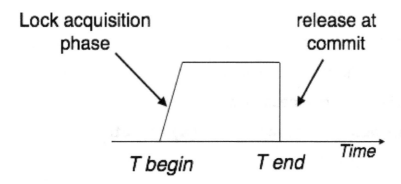

[Image: Strict Two Phase Locking]

Strict-2PL does not have cascading abort as 2PL does.

Timestamp-based Protocols

The most commonly used concurrency protocol is the timestamp based protocol. This protocol uses either system time or logical counter as a timestamp.

Lock-based protocols manage the order between the conflicting pairs among transactions at the time of execution, whereas timestamp-based protocols start working as soon as a transaction is created.

Every transaction has a timestamp associated with it, and the ordering is determined by the age of the transaction. A transaction created at 0002 clock time would be older than all other transactions that come after it. For example, any transaction 'y' entering the system at 0004 is two seconds younger and the priority would be given to the older one.

In addition, every data item is given the latest read and write-timestamp. This lets the system know when the last 'read and write' operation was performed on the data item.

Timestamp Ordering Protocol

The timestamp-ordering protocol ensures serializability among transactions in their conflicting read and write operations. This is the responsibility of the protocol system that the conflicting pair of tasks should be executed according to the timestamp values of the transactions.

- The timestamp of transaction T_i is denoted as $TS(T_i)$.

- Read timestamp of data-item X is denoted by R-timestamp(X).

- Write timestamp of data-item X is denoted by W-timestamp(X).

Timestamp ordering protocol works as follows:

- **If a transaction T_i issues a read(X) operation:**

  o If $TS(T_i) < $ W-timestamp(X)

- Operation rejected.
    - o If TS(T$_i$) >= W-timestamp(X)
        - Operation executed.
    - o All data-item timestamps updated.
- **If a transaction T$_i$ issues a write(X) operation:**
    - o If TS(T$_i$) < R-timestamp(X)
        - Operation rejected.
    - o If TS(T$_i$) < W-timestamp(X)
        - Operation rejected and T$_i$ rolled back.
    - o Otherwise, operation executed.

Thomas' Write Rule

This rule states if TS(Ti) < W-timestamp(X), then the operation is rejected and T$_i$ is rolled back.

Timestamp ordering rules can be modified to make the schedule view serializable.

Instead of making Ti rolled back, the 'write' operation itself is ignored.

22. DEADLOCK

In a multi-process system, deadlock is an unwanted situation that arises in a shared resource environment, where a process indefinitely waits for a resource that is held by another process.

For example, assume a set of transactions $\{T_0, T_1, T_2, ..., T_n\}$. T_0 needs a resource X to complete its task. Resource X is held by T_1, and T_1 is waiting for a resource Y, which is held by T_2. T_2 is waiting for resource Z, which is held by T_0. Thus, all the processes wait for each other to release resources. In this situation, none of the processes can finish their task. This situation is known as a deadlock.

Deadlocks are not healthy for a system. In case a system is stuck in a deadlock, the transactions involved in the deadlock are either rolled back or restarted.

Deadlock Prevention

To prevent any deadlock situation in the system, the DBMS aggressively inspects all the operations, where transactions are about to execute. The DBMS inspects the operations and analyzes if they can create a deadlock situation. If it finds that a deadlock situation might occur, then that transaction is never allowed to be executed.

There are deadlock prevention schemes that use timestamp ordering mechanism of transactions in order to predetermine a deadlock situation.

Wait-Die Scheme

In this scheme, if a transaction requests to lock a resource (data item), which is already held with a conflicting lock by another transaction, then one of the two possibilities may occur:

- If $TS(T_i) < TS(T_j)$ — that is T_i, which is requesting a conflicting lock, is older than T_j — then T_i is allowed to wait until the data-item is available.

- If $TS(T_i) > TS(t_j)$ — that is T_i is younger than T_j — then T_i dies. T_i is restarted later with a random delay but with the same timestamp.

This scheme allows the older transaction to wait but kills the younger one.

Wound-Wait Scheme

In this scheme, if a transaction requests to lock a resource (data item), which is already held with conflicting lock by another transaction, one of the two possibilities may occur:

- If $TS(T_i) < TS(T_j)$, then T_i forces T_j to be rolled back — that is T_i wounds T_j. T_j is restarted later with a random delay but with the same timestamp.

- If $TS(T_i) > TS(T_j)$, then T_i is forced to wait until the resource is available.

This scheme allows the younger transaction to wait; but when an older transaction requests an item held by a younger one, the older transaction forces the younger one to abort and release the item.

In both the cases, the transaction that enters the system at a later stage is aborted.

Deadlock Avoidance

Aborting a transaction is not always a practical approach. Instead, deadlock avoidance mechanisms can be used to detect any deadlock situation in advance. Methods like "wait-for graph" are available but they are suitable for only those systems where transactions are lightweight having fewer instances of resource. In a bulky system, deadlock prevention techniques may work well.

Wait-for Graph

This is a simple method available to track if any deadlock situation may arise. For each transaction entering into the system, a node is created. When a transaction T_i requests for a lock on an item, say X, which is held by some other transaction T_j, a directed edge is created from T_i to T_j. If T_j releases item X, the edge between them is dropped and T_i locks the data item.

The system maintains this wait-for graph for every transaction waiting for some data items held by others. The system keeps checking if there's any cycle in the graph.

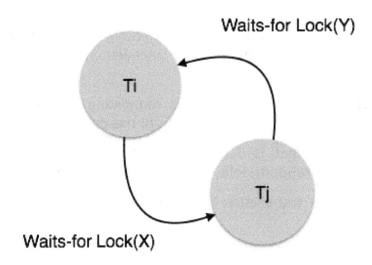

[*Image: Wait-for Graph*]

Here, we can use any of the two following approaches:

- First, do not allow any request for an item, which is already locked by another transaction. This is not always feasible and may cause starvation, where a transaction indefinitely waits for a data item and can never acquire it.

- The second option is to roll back one of the transactions. It is not always feasible to roll back the younger transaction, as it may be important than the older one. With the help of some relative algorithm, a transaction is chosen, which is to be aborted. This transaction is known as the **victim** and the process is known as **victim selection.**

23. DATA BACKUP

Loss of Volatile Storage

A volatile storage like RAM stores all the active logs, disk buffers, and related data. In addition, it stores all the transactions that are being currently executed. What happens if such a volatile storage crashes abruptly? It would obviously take away all the logs and active copies of the database. It makes recovery almost impossible, as everything that is required to recover the data is lost.

Following techniques may be adopted in case of loss of volatile storage:

- We can have **checkpoints** at multiple stages so as to save the contents of the database periodically.

- A state of active database in the volatile memory can be periodically **dumped** onto a stable storage, which may also contain logs and active transactions and buffer blocks.

- <dump> can be marked on a log file, whenever the database contents are dumped from a non-volatile memory to a stable one.

Recovery:

- When the system recovers from a failure, it can restore the latest dump.

- It can maintain a redo-list and an undo-list as checkpoints.

- It can recover the system by consulting undo-redo lists to restore the state of all transactions up to the last checkpoint.

Database Backup & Recovery from Catastrophic Failure

A catastrophic failure is one where a stable, secondary storage device gets corrupt. With the storage device, all the valuable data that is stored inside is lost. We have two different strategies to recover data from such a catastrophic failure:

- Remote backup – Here a backup copy of the database is stored at a remote location from where it can be restored in case of a catastrophe.

- Alternatively, database backups can be taken on magnetic tapes and stored at a safer place. This backup can later be transferred onto a freshly installed database to bring it to the point of backup.

Grown-up databases are too bulky to be frequently backed up. In such cases, we have techniques where we can restore a database just by looking at its logs. So, all that we need to do here is to take a backup of all the logs at frequent intervals of time. The database can be backed up once a week, and the logs being very small can be backed up every day or as frequently as possible.

Remote Backup

Remote backup provides a sense of security in case the primary location where the database is located gets destroyed. Remote backup can be offline or real-time or online. In case it is offline, it is maintained manually.

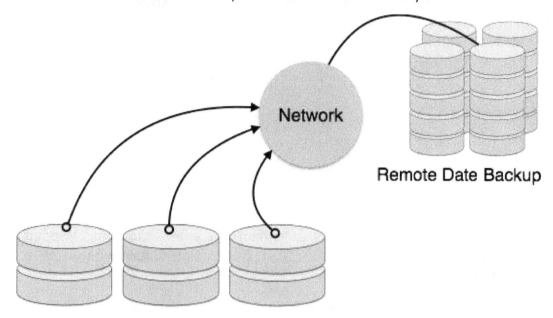

Remote Date Backup

Local Data Backup

[*Image: Remote Data Backup*]

Online backup systems are more real-time and lifesavers for database administrators and investors. An online backup system is a mechanism where every bit of the real-time data is backed up simultaneously at two distant places. One of them is directly connected to the system and the other one is kept at a remote place as backup.

As soon as the primary database storage fails, the backup system senses the failure and switches the user system to the remote storage. Sometimes this is so instant that the users can't even realize a failure.

24. DATA RECOVERY

Crash Recovery

DBMS is a highly complex system with hundreds of transactions being executed every second. The durability and robustness of a DBMS depends on its complex architecture and its underlying hardware and system software. If it fails or crashes amid transactions, it is expected that the system would follow some sort of algorithm or techniques to recover lost data.

Failure Classification

To see where the problem has occurred, we generalize a failure into various categories, as follows:

Transaction Failure

A transaction has to abort when it fails to execute or when it reaches a point from where it can't go any further. This is called transaction failure where only a few transactions or processes are hurt.

Reasons for a transaction failure could be:

- **Logical errors**: Where a transaction cannot complete because it has some code error or any internal error condition.

- **System errors**: Where the database system itself terminates an active transaction because the DBMS is not able to execute it, or it has to stop because of some system condition. For example, in case of deadlock or resource unavailability, the system aborts an active transaction.

System Crash

There are problems – external to the system – that may cause the system to stop abruptly and cause the system to crash. For example, interruptions in power supply may cause the failure of underlying hardware or software failure.

Examples may include operating system errors.

Disk Failure

In early days of technology evolution, it was a common problem where hard-disk drives or storage drives used to fail frequently.

Disk failures include formation of bad sectors, unreachability to the disk, disk head crash or any other failure, which destroys all or a part of disk storage.

Storage Structure

We have already described the storage system. In brief, the storage structure can be divided into two categories:

- **Volatile storage**: As the name suggests, a volatile storage cannot survive system crashes. Volatile storage devices are placed very close to the CPU; normally they are embedded onto the chipset itself. For example, main memory and cache memory are examples of volatile storage. They are fast but can store only a small amount of information.

- **Non-volatile storage**: These memories are made to survive system crashes. They are huge in data storage capacity, but slower in accessibility. Examples may include hard-disks, magnetic tapes, flash memory, and non-volatile (battery backed up) RAM.

Recovery and Atomicity

When a system crashes, it may have several transactions being executed and various files opened for them to modify the data items. Transactions are made of various operations, which are atomic in nature. But according to ACID properties of DBMS, atomicity of transactions as a whole must be maintained, that is, either all the operations are executed or none.

When a DBMS recovers from a crash, it should maintain the following:

- It should check the states of all the transactions, which were being executed.

- A transaction may be in the middle of some operation; the DBMS must ensure the atomicity of the transaction in this case.

- It should check whether the transaction can be completed now or it needs to be rolled back.

- No transactions would be allowed to leave the DBMS in an inconsistent state.

There are two types of techniques, which can help a DBMS in recovering as well as maintaining the atomicity of a transaction:

- Maintaining the logs of each transaction, and writing them onto some stable storage before actually modifying the database.

- Maintaining shadow paging, where the changes are done on a volatile memory, and later, the actual database is updated.

Log-based Recovery

Log is a sequence of records, which maintains the records of actions performed by a transaction. It is important that the logs are written prior to the actual modification and stored on a stable storage media, which is failsafe.

Log-based recovery works as follows:

- The log file is kept on a stable storage media.

- When a transaction enters the system and starts execution, it writes a log about it.

```
<Tn, Start>
```

- When the transaction modifies an item X, it write logs as follows:

```
<Tn, X, V1, V2>
```

It reads Tn has changed the value of X, from V1 to V2.

- When the transaction finishes, it logs:

```
<Tn, commit>
```

The database can be modified using two approaches:

- **Deferred database modification**: All logs are written on to the stable storage and the database is updated when a transaction commits.

- **Immediate database modification**: Each log follows an actual database modification. That is, the database is modified immediately after every operation.

Recovery with Concurrent Transactions

When more than one transaction are being executed in parallel, the logs are interleaved. At the time of recovery, it would become hard for the recovery system to backtrack all logs, and then start recovering. To ease this situation, most modern DBMS use the concept of 'checkpoints'.

Checkpoint

Keeping and maintaining logs in real time and in real environment may fill out all the memory space available in the system. As time passes, the log file may grow too big to be handled at all. Checkpoint is a mechanism where all the previous logs are removed from the system and stored permanently in a storage disk. Checkpoint declares a point before which the DBMS was in consistent state, and all the transactions were committed.

Recovery

When a system with concurrent transactions crashes and recovers, it behaves in the following manner:

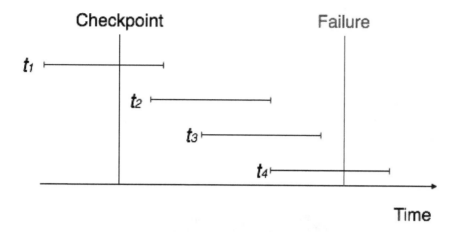

[Image: Recovery with concurrent transactions]

- The recovery system reads the logs backwards from the end to the last checkpoint.

- It maintains two lists, an undo-list and a redo-list.

- If the recovery system sees a log with $<T_n, Start>$ and $<T_n, Commit>$ or just $<T_n, Commit>$, it puts the transaction in the redo-list.

- If the recovery system sees a log with $<T_n, Start>$ but no commit or abort log found, it puts the transaction in the undo-list.

All the transactions in the undo-list are then undone and their logs are removed. All the transactions in the redo-list and their previous logs are removed and then redone before saving their logs.